Recognizing Media Bias and Disinformation

James Roland

ReferencePoint
Press

San Diego, CA

© 2024 ReferencePoint Press, Inc.
Printed in the United States

For more information, contact:
ReferencePoint Press, Inc.
PO Box 27779
San Diego, CA 92198
www.ReferencePointPress.com

LIBRARY OF CONGRESS CATALOGING-IN-PUBLICATION DATA

Names: Roland, James, author.
Title: Recognizing media bias and disinformation / by James Roland.
Description: San Diego : ReferencePoint Press, 2023. | Series: Developing
   digital and media literacy skills | Includes bibliographical references
   and index.
Identifiers: LCCN 2022058635 (print) | LCCN 2022058636 (ebook) | ISBN
   9781678205362 (library binding) | ISBN 9781678205379 (ebook)
Subjects: LCSH: Journalism--Objectivity--United States--Juvenile
   literature. | Mass media--Objectivity--United States--Juvenile
   literature. | Journalism--Political aspects--United States--Juvenile
   literature.
Classification: LCC PN4888.O25 R65 2023 (print) | LCC PN4888.O25 (ebook)
   | DDC 302.230973--dc23/eng/20230106
LC record available at https://lccn.loc.gov/2022058635
LC ebook record available at https://lccn.loc.gov/2022058636

CONTENTS

Be a Smarter News Consumer

During the frightening and confusing early weeks of the COVID-19 pandemic in 2020—a year before vaccines were available—a story started circulating on social media that boiling garlic cloves in seven cups of water and drinking it would cure a person infected by the COVID-19 virus. The story was being shared with people all around the globe and gained so much momentum that the World Health Organization finally had to make a formal statement that, while garlic has some healthy properties, it had not been proven to protect people from the virus.

In other words, what was viewed by many people as a helpful remedy endorsed by a seemingly large number of social media users was completely false. Many similar ineffective treatments as well as lies and half-truths about COVID-19 itself were circulated during those fearful times, and several continue to be shared today. In an age when unsupported claims can be shared so easily through social media and other forms of mass communication, it can be hard to know what to believe, especially when what looks or sounds like a legitimate news story is tainted with bias or is riddled with flat-out lies and disinformation. Such false information and bias seem to routinely follow the lives and actions of politicians, celebrities, and athletes, but they also distort people's perspectives on climate change, immigration, education, elections, crime, and many other serious topics that affect society as a whole.

Seeking the Truth

Media bias and disinformation are two different things, but they often share the same purpose: to manipulate how members of the public think and act rather than allow people to make up their own minds based on actual facts.

To avoid being manipulated by those trying to push an agenda or sell a product, it is vital that people learn to recognize examples of media bias and disinformation by seeking out the truth from reliable news outlets or other sources and ignoring unproven claims. That means being skeptical of claims or statements that seem suspect or come from sources that might have reasons to stray from the truth. And it might entail accepting something as false that you long believed to be true, or vice versa. In short, recognizing media bias and disinformation requires a willingness to think about the news and media you consume and do the extra work to make sure you have your facts straight.

These days it can be harder than ever to be a smart news consumer. The internet and social media allow actual news and disinformation to spread quickly around the world. Twenty-four-hour cable news channels are always looking to be the first with "breaking news," and websites desperate for clicks and attention can resort to running news stories without double-checking the facts or, in the worst case, making up stories to draw more viewers to their sites. When stories are moving so fast, many people do not take the time to confirm their accuracy, especially if the information is particularly colorful or sensational.

The Attraction of Misinformation and the Harms of Disinformation

Everyone likes a good story, and research has shown that false news travels faster than the facts. A study led by researchers at the Massachusetts Institute of Technology (MIT) found that false news spread much more quickly on Twitter than real news. "False news is more novel, and people are more likely to share novel information,"[1] says Sinan Aral, a professor at the MIT Sloan School of Management and coauthor of the study published in the journal *Science*. He adds that spreading new information, whether it is true or not, makes people feel like they are in the know and up-to-date with the latest news.

But this desire to be first with the story and share juicy gossip can lead to problems big and small. Rumors and misinformation can ruin reputations, trigger violence, divide families and friends, create chaos, and make the people who spread lies and distort the truth less trustworthy and potentially guilty of crimes or liable for the harm inflicted by their lies. *Mis*information is erroneous or unintentionally misleading; *dis*information is intended to deceive or sow doubt about generally trustworthy facts or institutions. For example, Alex Jones, who hosts an internet show based on news commentary and conspiracy theories, was ordered by

Alex Jones takes the stand to testify during his Sandy Hook defamation trial in Waterbury, Connecticut, on September 22, 2022. Jones has spent years claiming the shooting was staged and that no one was really killed.

the courts to pay more than $1 billion to families of victims shot in the 2012 Sandy Hook Elementary School massacre that left twenty children and six staff members dead. Jones, who regularly rails against the mainstream media and claims there are secret operatives in the federal government plotting a government takeover, spent years falsely claiming that the shooting was staged and the grieving parents were actors.

And while most cases of disinformation and media bias are not as extreme as Jones's behavior, it is nevertheless essential that people remain vigilant in their efforts to seek the truth and slow or stop the spread of potentially harmful lies. In a 2022 interview with ABC News, John Jackson, dean of the University of Pennsylvania's Annenberg School for Communication, urged news consumers to be careful in processing and sharing new information. "The internet allows people to create their own evidence from scratch, and then spread it to millions of others," he says. "That doesn't mean their evidence means anything, but it does mean that we all have to be better at evaluating what they're saying."[2]

> "The internet allows people to create their own evidence from scratch, and then spread it to millions of others. That doesn't mean their evidence means anything, but it does mean that we all have to be better at evaluating what they're saying."[2]
>
> —John Jackson, dean of the University of Pennsylvania's Annenberg School for Communication

CHAPTER ONE

What Is News?

Simply put, news is a report on recent events, such as a wildfire or a protest for social justice, or an analysis of current situations, such as climate change or inflation. The news media that deliver this information include network and cable television, radio, newspapers, and magazines—as well as the online versions of these news operations—plus blogs, podcasts, web-only news sites, and social media.

News outlets are how most people learn about their communities and the world. And because their job is so important, the news media should be held to a high standard. People want to know what is really going on, so there is an expectation that news articles and stories on TV and the internet will be accurate. Lynn Walsh, an investigative reporter and former president of the Society for Professional Journalists, wrote that most journalists take the obligation to cover the news with objectivity and fairness very seriously. She adds, however, that most stories are not simply a list of straightforward, indisputable facts. Good journalism requires putting events into context and finding a compelling angle to take on a story, and it should be understood that no two reporters will cover a story in the same way. All people—including journalists—bring a lifetime of experiences and perspectives that may shape how they interpret an event or an issue. "Journalists not only provide a window to the world, they provide many windows to the world," Walsh wrote in a column for the *Orlando Sentinel*. "Each may vary from another, but ethical and responsible journalists will make sure people get the most accurate view possible."[3]

Unfortunately, there are plenty of news stories that contain opinions, not just facts, or present information in a way that is slanted toward a particular point of a view. And in the worst cases, some news stories contain outright lies or deliberately misleading information. But examples of media bias include much more than the words or pictures in a story. Information that is left out of a story, how much attention a story gets, or even the decision not to cover a story on a certain subject or event are all examples of how news outlets can manipulate the information consumers receive or fail to receive. To recognize media bias and disinformation, it helps to understand more about the media and the way news stories are selected and presented to the public.

Packaging the News

With a few variations, the fundamental components of a news story are essentially the same for print, broadcast, and online news. Print and online news stories usually lead with a headline that sums up the main point of an article. Then the article itself will include direct quotes, paraphrased quotes, and information that may or may not be attributed to its source. In addition, images typically accompany the written copy, and these might include photos, charts, maps, and illustrations in print media. Online versions of these stories can include video as well. Television news stories do not contain a headline and words to be read by viewers, but instead feature a news anchor or reporter telling a story, often accompanied by video and on-camera interviews with sources. Television and many streaming news sources have the advantage of covering breaking news as it is happening, often on the scene of the event.

All print, television, and online news operations have editors, producers, or news directors who oversee newsrooms and make decisions about what stories to cover. Reporters and photographers are assigned to stories. Once those assignments have been completed, the stories are packaged for public consumption in a daily newspaper, TV newscast, online news site, or other outlet. While "big" stories like a presidential election or an earthquake get most of the attention, most stories that fill your digital news feeds, a local or network TV newscast, or a daily newspaper address a wide range of topics that editors and news directors believe are important for the public to know about, even if simply interesting or entertaining. A space probe sending back pictures of Pluto, for example, may not affect the family budget or upcoming election, but it does capture the imagination.

In addition to which news stories are covered, how they are presented can often be the first sign of possible media bias. Stories a news outlet considers most important are located above the fold in traditional newspapers or at the top of an online news feed. Television newscasts present the most important stories first, while stories considered less important are presented later.

The Definition of Newsworthy

How a news organization decides what constitutes a newsworthy event or topic varies from newsroom to newsroom and is shaped by the news organization's mission. A local paper will devote resources to covering the city council, road construction, high school sports, and the county fair because its readers turn to that paper for such information. But a larger paper in that region or a national paper like *USA Today* or the *Wall Street Journal* needs to reach a broader audience, so they cannot give the same amount of space to community news.

But all newsrooms, even online-only news sites like HuffPost or BuzzFeed, have daily meetings of editors, reporters, columnists, photographers, and other journalists to discuss and often debate what to cover, whether it is breaking news or feature stories that will run in the future. Those decisions shape not only the information that reaches much of the public but also how news organizations are viewed. Determining what is or is not newsworthy opens journalists up to a lot of criticism and accusations of bias.

Throughout the campaign and presidency of Donald Trump, journalists constantly found themselves questioning whether or how much to cover the president's tweets. On any given day, Trump might use Twitter to criticize a member of Congress, announce a policy change, brag about his poll numbers, or complain about his news coverage, often referring to the press as "the enemy of the people."[4]

Many journalists refused to address those tweets in their news reporting, contending that chasing after every random thought shared on Twitter was not good journalism. Others, however, knew that the more incendiary tweets would attract the most readers or viewers—and so they covered the tweets. For instance, in a November 2016 tweet, Trump complained about the cast of *Hamilton* addressing Vice President-Elect Mike Pence, who was attending their performance. Cast members expressed their concern that the new administration would not protect the environment and the rights of people from all walks of life. The *Hamilton* incident and Trump's response became one of the big news stories of the day and was emblematic of the challenge facing journalists: Should Trump's every tweet or offhand comment be treated as newsworthy? Even before Trump took office, journalists were debating the issue. On NBC's *Meet the Press* in early 2017, magazine writer and author Gabriel Sherman said:

> The fact that he's tweeting is not news at this point. I mean, we've got to cover what the president-elect and the president says. But the fact that he's going to say something outrageous that then becomes the focus of the coverage I think is abdicating the role, which is the media should be setting the agenda and deciding what is the news. And yes, when the president says something we cover it. But we should not just be ping ponging back and forth from his tweets.[5]

There are not always right or wrong answers to questions about whether something is newsworthy or, if it is deemed newsworthy, how best to cover it. A news outlet can reveal its bias by giving certain stories more prominence or, conversely, giving them less attention or ignoring them completely, depending on that outlet's agenda. For example, on June 9, 2022, when the US House of Representatives' Select Committee held its first televised hearings concerning the January 6, 2021, storming of the Capitol by pro-Trump supporters, most major networks—such as CNN, ABC, CBS, and NBC—covered the prime-time proceedings live. The networks believed there was significant public interest and importance regarding the lawmakers' investigation into the attempt to disrupt Congress's efforts to certify the votes from the presidential election two months before. But one major news channel, Fox News, skipped the live coverage and aired its usual lineup of conservative commentators, who used most of their time to criticize the hearing as liberal propaganda and downplay the event's connection to the conservative president. Fox News and the other networks did air some of the hearings that were held during the day in the months that followed. However, Fox News continued to use its prime-time lineup of commentators to criticize the committee and its parade of witness testimony.

Fox News's decision not to broadcast the first big January 6 committee hearing drew heavy criticism from many observers, but these kinds of choices are made by news organizations every day, usually without much attention from beyond the newsroom.

Trump supporters storm the US Capitol on January 6, 2021. Most major networks aired live coverage of the House of Representatives' June 2022 hearings on the event, but Fox News notably did not.

Bylines and Accountability

When assessing a news article for accuracy and bias, it is always a good idea to look for a byline. This is the name of the person (or persons) who wrote the article. If there is no byline, it suggests that no one is taking responsibility for its content, and that should be a red flag that it may contain lies or at least some misinformation. "Bylines are sacred—they ensure accountability, reward good writing, and punish recklessness," says Ted Fraser, a reporter for the *Toronto Star*, a Canadian newspaper.

There are legitimate occasions when a byline is not used. Sometimes content is compiled by newsroom staff or the article is really a news brief that the news organization does not think warrants a byline. But for a major story, especially one that includes biased language, look to see who is credited. If a byline is present and it is linked, see where the link takes you. Learning more about the writer can also be helpful in deciding whether it is a reliable source. Look for other articles written by the author or for a LinkedIn profile or other biographical information. The more you know about who is delivering the news, the better able you will be to determine its fairness and legitimacy.

Ted Fraser, "To Understand the History of Journalism, Look Down," Medium, April 7, 2019. https://medium.com.

But noting how news is or is not covered can alert you to possible bias. One easy test is to see whether a story is covered by multiple news organizations or just one. If a story gets a lot of attention from different news organizations, then it is probably a legitimate news item. But if other respected news organizations do not pick it up, be suspicious about whether the item is newsworthy or just a tidbit blown up to push a biased agenda.

The "Both Sides" Challenge

It is easy to argue that all reporting is biased because of the political leanings of the news outlet and the choices its directors make in how and when they disclose information. However, sometimes media bias occurs unintentionally when journalists are actually trying to be unbiased. Telling a fair, thorough, and accurate news story usually demands that reporters include a mix of perspectives on the main subject of their story. The concept is not unique to journalism. If there is a fight at school, teachers and administrators will talk to all the students involved to try to find out what happened and how it started. In a courtroom, people accused of a crime can mount a defense against the charges facing them. In this way, both sides of a story are presented in court. It would not be fair, for example, if a judge and jury heard only from the prosecution.

When gathering the news, reporters who do not want to appear biased may try to give equal space in a story to opposing voices. But there are many instances in which one side's argument or opinion simply does not carry equal weight to the other, or more problematically, offers misinformation. This is a common problem in covering subjects such as climate change. A reporter might interview scientists whose research suggests a real urgency in addressing greenhouse gases and other causes of climate problems. But to be "fair," the reporter may also interview someone who disagrees with the research or with the need to address climate change at all, even when it is clear that this view is held by only a handful of scientists.

In the end, the article may end up giving equal space to both sides, despite one side having the preponderance of facts, research, and evidence to back up its claims, while the other side offers no vetted claims or opinions. Northwestern University researcher David Rapp calls situations like this a "false balance."[6] He conducted a study that highlighted the simple truth that not all sides of every argument are equally valid. He suggested that one way to resolve the problem is for journalists to include the consensus view on a topic rather than pit one person against the other in a news story. In the case of climate change or any other controversial topic, a responsible news story would point out the number of scientists who agree about the urgency to protect the planet. "Climate change is a great case study of the false balance problem, because the scientific consensus is nearly unanimous. If 99 doctors said you needed surgery to save your life, but one disagreed, chances are you'd listen to the 99," Rapp said in an article on the website Northwestern Now. "But we often see one climate scientist pitted against one climate denier or down player, as if it's a 50-50 split."[7]

Paying close attention to and even checking up on the sources quoted in a story and the merits of their statements and arguments can help you come to your own conclusions about a subject and whether a particular media outlet is pushing one side or another. But sometimes you can get a pretty good idea of what the story will be like just based on the headline.

Headlines and Clickbait

The first thing a person usually reads in a news story is the headline. When scrolling through a digital news feed or skimming a newspaper or magazine, readers scan the headlines. If a story seems interesting, then a reader might move beyond the headline and read all or part of the article associated with that headline. Television newscasts do not use headlines in the same way, but they do have "teasers," which can be a sentence or two an anchor reads about an upcoming story to keep viewers watching.

But headlines can be tricky, because they must be fairly short yet sum up the main point of a news story. That is not easy with a complicated subject, but it is important because a headline might be all that a person reads and may make the difference between a person stopping to read the article or moving right past it. Because news outlets want readers, headlines can often be sensationalized or even misleading in an effort to attract attention.

Dr. Robert H. Shmerling, senior faculty editor at Harvard Health Publishing, wrote about the many problems and challenges related to health and medical news headlines. He noted that words such as *breakthrough* and *groundbreaking* are often used, yet true breakthroughs in medical research are rare, since progress in developing new treatments tends to happen gradually. Another misleading practice is the omission of important facts about a study. Many studies are performed on animals, but headlines usually leave out that detail, leaving readers to assume that research findings about a new medication, for example, are applicable to humans. "Leaving out this important detail from the headline exaggerates the study's importance," Shmerling wrote on Harvard Health Publishing's *Staying Healthy*

Interviewing 101

When watching an interview online or on TV, you can learn a lot about the interviewer by what questions are asked and those that should be asked but are not. A good reporter conducts an interview to learn what the interview subject thinks and feels about an event or topic. The questions should be tough but fair, not simply invitations to spout unchallenged claims or propaganda. A good interviewer will notice whether the person being interviewed says something unexpected or something that demands a follow-up question.

If an elected official makes an outrageous claim about a political rival or a rival's policy, it is up to the interviewer to ask follow-up questions. This might mean asking for elaboration, clarification, or evidence. This is an important part of the reporter's job. "Asking tough questions—you know, that's what we do. They get mad. We have to do our jobs. They don't like being pressed when there are scandals. And as long as you're respectful and have your facts right, you push ahead," longtime NBC News reporter Andrea Mitchell said in a 2019 interview. If an interviewer lets a bombshell comment go by without stopping to ask a follow-up question, the interviewer either is not a great journalist or is perhaps protecting the interview subject.

Quoted in Terry Gross, "Journalist Andrea Mitchell: Asking Tough Questions Is 'Very Empowering,'" *Fresh Air*, NPR, September 18, 2019. www.npr.org.

blog. "In a world of misleading health news headlines, here's my advice: be skeptical. Consider the source and read past the headline before buying in. And if your go-to media often serves up misleading headlines, consider changing channels or crossing that news source off your list."[8]

Misleading headlines can appear anywhere, but they seem to flourish online. Some types of digital headlines are referred to as "clickbait," because they use shocking or dramatic language to lure readers to click on the story. The article under a clickbait headline may be a legitimate news story, but the nature of its headline may not quite match the tone or thrust of the news within the story. And sometimes the article itself or an eye-catching photograph can be considered clickbait because they have little real news value.

> "If your go-to media often serves up misleading headlines, consider changing channels or crossing that news source off your list."[8]
>
> —Robert H. Shmerling, senior faculty editor at Harvard Health Publishing

The reason online news sources turn to clickbait for their stories is because they track every click—each time someone opens that story on their computer or smartphone. More clicks means more users, which the companies can then show advertisers. More eyes on articles means more eyes on the ads around them, and more ads means more revenue. But more importantly, other than being a waste of time, clickbait items can sometimes be traps that put your devices and personal information at risk. The Better Business Bureau (BBB) issued a warning in 2020 after the death of Kobe Bryant, as scammers flooded the internet with fake articles promising new information about his death and with fake ads for Bryant memorabilia. The BBB explained that scammers often exploit tragedies or other major news events, and it urged consumers to avoid sites that promise "shocking" or "never before seen" video or information. "Once clicked, the reader is taken to a site that may

Kobe Bryant (right) faces LeBron James during an NBA game on February 10, 2013. After Bryant's death in 2020, scammers flooded the internet with fake articles and ads related to the sports superstar.

allow cyber criminals to hijack your account or steal personal information,"[9] the BBB warned.

Being conscious of clickbait and other deceptive practices can help you become a better news consumer. Knowing that specific news outlets or authors often have agendas and may be willing to provide unbalanced reporting or clearly skewed interpretations also makes you aware of how to sort through bias, verify sources, and check facts. These efforts will make you better informed and able to justify your own opinions on important news topics.

CHAPTER TWO

Biased Language and Spin

Everybody has bias for or against something. Sports fans favor their team or player and often criticize their rivals. That sort of partiality is usually fun and harmless. But when it comes to the news, media bias can be problematic, especially if news consumers are not fully aware of how much prejudice and partisanship are influencing what they read and hear.

Media bias can be blatant or subtle. Showing an unflattering or embarrassing photo of a famous person alongside a headline or caption that further insults the individual is blatant media bias. Those types of examples are easy to recognize. But often media bias can be harder to detect. It is revealed in the use of certain words or the way opinion overlaps with facts and objective information. Recognizing media bias or the way news makers try to spin their messages is helpful in getting at the truth and not being taken advantage of by people trying to manipulate the way you think and feel.

News vs. Opinion

For many years, broadcast news and newspapers were the main sources of news for most people. And those news outlets made a point of differentiating between their news and their opinion content. Newspaper articles are meant to be objective, factual, and free of bias and opinion. Most newspapers also devote at least one page, and often two or more, to editorials and op-ed pieces (so named because they appear opposite the editorials). Op-ed pieces are opinion columns written by a variety of people, including nationally syndicated columnists as well as local and national figures such as politicians, medical experts, retired military leaders, religious figures, educators, and so on.

Editorials are written by the newspaper's editorial writers, who usually work in offices separate from the newsroom to preserve some independence and avoid the appearance of influencing news coverage. Editorials tend to focus on issues of broad concern, such as how elected officials should deal with an important topic like school safety or raising taxes. Many newspapers still endorse specific candidates running for office. Editorials and op-ed pieces have one purpose: to convince readers of the best solution, course of action, or assessment of a particular situation. Editorials are usually run without a byline and are presented as the opinions of the paper's editorial staff only, not the editors and reporters who fill the news sections of the paper.

Network and local television newscasts used to refrain from presenting their version of editorials or opinions. When they did, the news anchor would make a point of turning things over to someone else to deliver what was clearly explained to be an opinion, not straight news. These segments were called commentaries and were limited to a few minutes at most in a thirty-minute newscast.

But with the rise of twenty-four-hour news channels such as CNN, Fox News, and MSNBC, the line between news and opinion started to blur in the 1990s. News anchors began hosting roundtable discussions, which feature experts or other journalists who are there specifically to analyze the top stories of the day. These discussions often include considerable amounts of opinion, not just objective analysis. Experts and analysts, referred to as pundits, often come to such programs from politics. Former elected officials, White House press secretaries, and other well-known political figures are interviewed for their interpretation of events or speculation about upcoming elections, court cases, and the like. Keep this mind when you listen to someone analyze the news. If they represented a political party, chances are they will continue to be a voice for the opinions they held in office rather than offer unbiased viewpoints.

In the early 2000s certain news channels began presenting programs hosted by someone who appears to be a news anchor but is a mouthpiece for a very specific point of view on the news. Even when the show hosts interview someone, the person being interviewed is there either to agree with or support the host's opinion or to be asked leading questions that can further the host's viewpoint. When people with opposing views are inter-

Newsrooms are bustling places where many journalists work side by side to produce stories. Editorial writers often work separately to avoid the appearance of influencing news coverage.

viewed, they are often ridiculed for making counterarguments to the points the host is trying to make.

These talk show personalities have succeeded in obscuring the line between news and opinion, says Frank Sesno, a former CNN anchor and former director of George Washington University's School of Media and Public Affairs. "One of the dangers is thinking that people know the difference between the editorial page and the front page, between a commentator or pundit commenting on something alongside a reporter who's supposed to be providing facts. In this environment, when you have news, talking points and opinions all colliding, it can be really disorienting to the audience."[10]

The key distinction between news and opinion is that a straight news story exists to inform readers or viewers with objective, balanced information, not to sway them to one side of an issue. An opinion piece or commentary may include facts and reporting, but the tone of the content and the point it is trying to make are clearly coming from one point of view and are likely to reveal the person's biases. Opinion pieces aim only to get others to think and feel the same as the person behind the editorial or commentary.

"One of the dangers is thinking that people know the difference between the editorial page and the front page, between a commentator or pundit commenting on something alongside a reporter who's supposed to be providing facts."[10]

—Frank Sesno, former director of George Washington University's School of Media and Public Affairs

Biased Language

The specific words used to express an idea or feeling or to relay information can make all the difference in how those ideas, feelings, and information are received.

Journalists, advertisers, and other members of the media are aware of how certain words carry different meanings or connotations even if they have similar definitions. This is how bias works its way into the news, often in subtle ways that do not necessarily jump out at readers or viewers. For example, if a person in a story "admits" something, it implies that he or she did something wrong

Worth a Thousand Words

The saying "a picture is worth a thousand words" means that a single photo or illustration often can tell a story or express ideas even better than the written word. Freelance photojournalist Claire Thomas says that news photos capturing accurate images of events and subjects are especially helpful in an era when words and speech cannot always be trusted. "I think photojournalism is as important as ever, especially given how quickly and easily false information can spread nowadays," she said in a 2021 interview.

The choice of a particular image to accompany a news story can say a lot about the opinions or feelings of the editors or whoever was responsible for selecting it. If a photo of a politician is especially flattering, for example, the article will probably also be flattering. If the photo shows the person yelling, looking confused, or in an unflattering pose, the article will likely not portray the individual in a good light. An image that is neutral suggests that the article might not be biased one way or the other. Noting the pairing of images and articles can thus be another way to assess bias or objectivity.

Quoted in Nezih Tavlas, "I Want My Photos to Simply Convey an Accurate Reflection of the Truth," Photojournalism News, November 3, 2021. www.photojournalismnews.com.

or was wrong about a previous statement or position he or she took. The same is true for words like *acknowledged* or *conceded*. The use of words like these instead of *said* or *says* suggests that bias may be at work.

Also, consider phrases such as "refused to say" or "declined to comment." On the surface, a reader might assume that a person was given the chance to answer a question or give a comment and chose not to do so because the person has something to hide. In some cases that is true. However, there could be several less-suspicious explanations. The individual involved may have chosen not to comment because he or she did not want to respond to an inappropriate question or was advised not to comment by a lawyer for legal reasons. Or the person may never have heard the question or been presented with the opportunity to comment yet in the story was portrayed as "refusing" or "declining" to comment. As a news consumer, you cannot always know the story behind the story and what the reporter did or did not do in putting the story together. However, sticking to the facts as much as possible and withholding judgment about things that are not clear in a story can help keep you from being swayed by bias in the news.

Of course, there are even more obvious words used in place of *said*, such as *bragged* or *fumed*. Sometimes these and other descriptive words accurately reflect how something was said or how a person was acting. Just be aware that the use of dramatic language is a common element of biased news coverage. Conversely, someone may have screamed an answer, for example, but if the reporter is biased toward that individual, the comment may be downplayed as something merely "said" or "replied." This is why it can be helpful to read more than one account of an event to see how different journalists cover it. Examining the different ways the same event is covered can be helpful in recognizing media bias because you can compare the language and images used by various news outlets.

These two publications are covering the same event—the US Supreme Court's June 24, 2022, decision to overturn the landmark case Roe v. Wade—but they take very different angles in presenting the information.

Debunking Fake News

With a seemingly unending stream of false information in the media, you may find yourself wondering how to separate fact from fiction. There are several reliable sites you can visit to see whether a story that seems suspicious has been proved true or debunked as false. The people who run these sites take their jobs very seriously because they know the average citizen deserves accurate information. "Mis- and disinformation circulates very fast in every crisis and one of the ways to limit its impact is to debunk it as quickly as possible," says Clara Jiménez Cruz, founder of the international Spanish-language fact-checking organization Maldita.es.

Reliable sites include FactCheck.org and Snopes. Both sites are well-respected, independent entities with no political or social bias. FactCheck.org, a project of the University of Pennsylvania's Annenberg Public Policy Center, tends to focus more on current issues and topics related to government and politics. Brief articles recap the claims being made and then assess whether they are true, false, or somewhere in between. Snopes takes a similar approach, but it also evaluates controversies in history. Both sites also seek to prove whether certain photographs or viral videos are real.

Quoted in Eduardo Suárez, "Cutting Through the Fog of War: How Fact-Checkers from 70 Countries Are Fighting Misinformation on Ukraine," Reuters Institute, March 21, 2022. https://reutersinstitute.politics.ox.ac.uk.

Comparing how events or issues are covered by reporters or discussed by pundits and commentators can help you spot examples of bias that you may never have considered. In recent years the use of *riot* and *protest* to describe the same event has prompted considerable discussion and debate among journalists, activists, politicians, and others. A riot is a violent and chaotic disturbance by a crowd. A protest is an organized, peaceful expression of disapproval by an individual or group. A collective protest can turn violent and chaotic, but labeling an otherwise peaceful event a "riot" simply because it involves a large, vocal crowd or because a few people in that crowd become aggressive is an example of bias. Professor of law and African American studies john a. powell (he does not capitalize his name) of the

University of California, Berkeley, told a *Time* magazine reporter in the summer of 2020, when social justice marches and rallies took place around the world, that the use of the word *riot* by certain journalists undercut the message of those protests. He said, "*Riot* suggests pandemonium. What's happening across the country and across the world is a call for justice, a call for police accountability, for the recognition that black lives matter too. *Rioting* detracts from all of that."[11]

The next time a big event is covered by multiple news outlets, pay attention to the headlines, the language, and the pictures and video that are used to see which organizations inject spin into their coverage and which try to be as objective as possible. And while you are looking for examples of bias, learn to identify the news organizations that rely on responsible, evenhanded wording to tell their stories.

Responsible Language

Responsible journalism also means reporters should not jump to conclusions and use terminology that will have readers and viewers making inaccurate or unfair judgments. If a person claims to have been attacked but there has been no proof provided publicly, then that person is an alleged victim. Once it has been confirmed that an attack took place, then that person could rightly be called a victim. Likewise, a person accused of the attack should be referred to as the alleged attacker (or alleged perpetrator or similar terms). If that person is convicted or admits guilt, then the term *alleged* or *accused* can be dropped. But assuming that a person accused of a crime is guilty without any legal proceedings is irresponsible. A news item that makes an assumption, such as the guilt of an accused person, without any confirmation may be biased and may contain other examples of slanted coverage.

In addition to using accurate, noninflammatory language, responsible journalists try not to misrepresent, oversimplify, or needlessly complicate a subject. While it is important to give the public plenty of information, it is also necessary to do so in a way that readers and viewers can understand. Responsible journalists focus on accuracy, verifying information before using it in a story. And when a mistake is made, good journalists do what they can to correct it. One of the great advantages of online news, as opposed to print or live television news, is that it can be updated as new information becomes available, either to fix a mistake or make the story more comprehensive. News outlets that take a cautious, responsible approach to sensitive stories are more likely to be fair and trustworthy.

The Bias of News Consumers

The issue of media bias is not just a matter of journalists putting spin on the news. The consumers of news play a role, too. Often accusations of bias are hurled by people who have strong feel-

Many news consumers turn to online sources for information. Unlike printed sources, online content can be updated as new information becomes available, providing up-to-the-minute facts and developments.

ings on an issue and believe that any coverage that gives "the other side" any legitimacy is biased or unbalanced.

But it is not just angry, vocal individuals railing against the media who feel this way. In a 2020 study conducted by the Pew Research Center, 79 percent of Americans said that news organizations tend to favor one side when presenting the news on political and social issues. Only one in five people believed news organizations usually treat these topics fairly and give appropriate space and time to all sides. In that same study, more than 90 percent of Republicans said the media unfairly favors one side on these issues, while 69 percent of Democrats expressed those same feelings. And even though conservatives often contend that journalists in the mainstream media are too liberal (research suggests that a majority of mainstream journalists actually do hold more liberal views than the general public), research suggests that personal political and social views tend not to creep into their coverage. In a 2020 study published in the journal *Science Advances*, researchers from three universities found that there was no evidence of liberal bias in the stories political journalists produce.

Assuming news coverage is biased without really analyzing it is more cynical than actually biased, and it often keeps people from getting a variety of perspectives on current events. Ironically, many consumers themselves approach the news with a biased point of view, even though they accuse the media of doing the same thing. The term *confirmation bias* refers to the tendency to consume news and information that further supports previously held beliefs. For example, people who distrust the safety and effectiveness of vaccines are more likely to consume news stories that are equally critical of and skeptical about vaccines.

Confirmation bias, while quite common, is unproductive in many respects because it prevents people from opening their minds and considering alternative points of view. The result is a society in which many people cannot even agree on basic facts and the truth, according to Jonathan Kaufman, director of Northeastern University's School of Journalism. "When you ask readers, viewers and listeners about bias, they all say they would like to see more nonpartisan news," Kaufman said in an interview with the university's news website staff. "But their reading and viewing habits are still the same, which is that, now more than ever, people are going to the news sources that reinforce what they think rather than challenge it, and I'm not sure people's behavior is going to change."[12]

CHAPTER THREE

Disinformation

Just as information is meant to educate and enlighten a person, disinformation serves the opposite purpose: to fool or deceive people, usually with the goal of making them think and act in a particular way. Disinformation can come from politicians, companies, and even individuals deliberately trying to confuse or keep the truth from the public.

Sometimes disinformation can be identified with a little research. But as digital technology such as Adobe Photoshop and even more-high-tech faking of videos become more sophisticated, it has become more difficult to separate fact from fiction. As always, news consumers are responsible for checking the source of potential disinformation, taking the time to confirm the facts, and not blindly accepting misleading stories and falsehoods.

Disinformation vs. Misinformation

Disinformation is not the same as misinformation, even though they sound similar and refer to inaccurate information. *Misinformation* refers to information that includes mistakes or inaccuracies that were generated or spread innocently, though some misinformation might be spread with the intent to deceive. Rumors or unsubstantiated news reports can also be considered misinformation if they turn out to be false.

Sometimes misinformation is the result of a misunderstanding or a misinterpretation of events or policies. People spreading misinformation may sincerely believe that the information they are sharing is accurate. In the 2022 midterm elections, the ballot in Connecticut contained an early voting initiative that would remove the required seal from certain ballots being submitted to the secretary of state for formal approval of election results. What the initiative was really doing was eliminating a centuries-old requirement that the election results had to be sealed with hot wax—a step that had not been done in a long time. But many concerned citizens interpreted the wording of the proposed ballot measure as a change that would affect the security of elections and began to spread this misinformation. *USA Today* picked up on the social media outrage about Connecticut's ballot initiative and conducted a fact-check, which it soon published and included in the newspaper's Twitter feed. "The more times people see or hear misinformation, the harder it becomes to set the record straight,"[13] *USA Today*'s senior director Kristen DelGuzzi notes.

Disinformation is always intended to hide the truth or deceive the public, and it can take many forms. Partisan journalists may repeat information that has already been debunked, sometimes by couching it as "people are saying . . ." to shift responsibility off themselves for spreading falsehoods. Disinformation also pops up on websites that traffic in conspiracy theories. Disinformation gets easily shared on social media and mainstream media outlets by so-called bad actors hoping to get more people to buy into the lies.

Disinformation may be something that makes a person look more accomplished, like lying on a résumé. Or disinformation can be something aimed at making a person or group of people look bad. Critics and opponents of President Barack Obama spent years accusing him of being born in Africa and thus not eligible for the presidency, even though records proved that he was born in Hawaii. Former Soviet leader Vladimir Lenin once said, "A lie told often enough becomes the truth."[14] And while that is not technically the case, plenty of people who knowingly spread disinformation want their falsehoods and exaggerations to be accepted as true.

Michigan State University (MSU) researcher Johannes Bauer explains that misinformation and disinformation easily spread because most of what people know about the world is assembled from what they read, view, observe on their own, and pick up in conversation. But it is always an incomplete picture. And because people want to fill in the picture as much as possible and feel informed, there is a tendency to believe what they hear or see without questioning the source of that information. Furthermore, people do not always question individuals or institutions that seem to have authority. We put trust in universities, police

Despite producing his birth certificate proving that he was born in Hawaii, former US president Barack Obama faced persistent accusations that he had been born in Africa and was thus ineligible for the presidency.

departments, news outlets, and politicians because we assume they are acting in the public good. Without trusting in some institutions or individuals, anchors for our own belief in truth can be difficult to secure. In an interview with the university's news site, Bauer said, "For example, a medical doctor typically knows more about diseases than a patient. We often 'patch' the parts we do not know by trusting others, trusting media, or by using our own problem-solving skills to determine what might be closest to 'truth.' This incompleteness opens a crack, through which misinformation and disinformation may come in."[15]

The solution to stopping or slowing the spread of disinformation is to evaluate and verify information as much as possible, even if it comes from a source that you consider reliable. It is also necessary at times to be skeptical of news or advertising claims that seem hard to believe, especially if they are made by sources that you do not know much about.

Fake News

However, it can be just as important to be skeptical of people urging you not to believe something that appears to be true or that you know to be true. The term *fake news* has become more widely used in recent years, usually by politicians who slap that label on articles that portray them or their policies in a bad light. Even if the reporting is accurate, coverage can still be called fake news, and people who support that politician will likely agree.

Former president Donald Trump often used the term *fake news* to describe unflattering coverage by mainstream media. He criticized many media outlets as promoting liberal agendas, and he also famously called reporters "the enemy of the people."[16] Many of his supporters echoed this distrust of journalism, and the furor left many observers wondering whether undermining the profession would damage the notion of a free press. And though the term *fake news* is frequently assigned to news that is true, there are enough examples of news stories that are fake that the public might simply accept that all media is untrustworthy. Indeed, a 2021 Gallup poll found that only 36 percent of Americans trust the media to report the news fully, accurately, and fairly.

If people feel they cannot trust the news, which is where they get most of their information about what is going on in the world, they might lose faith in other institutions in society. They will believe instead in the things they want to be true—regardless of whether they are true—and the result will be a society filled with people who cannot agree on the facts and who have no trust in government, schools, or other institutions that need public trust to operate, explains Bauer. He adds:

> "A broader, and more concerning, effect is that misinformation and disinformation undermine trust in elections, their outcomes, the media system reporting on elections and the broader political and governmental institutions that any prosperous, peaceful society needs."[17]
>
> —Johannes Bauer, Michigan State University researcher

A broader, and more concerning, effect is that misinformation and disinformation undermine trust in elections, their outcomes, the media system reporting on elections and the broader political and governmental institutions that any prosperous, peaceful society needs. This could result in long-term damage to our country's ability to solve the most challenging economic and social problems, which often require finding common ground. People need to be able to talk to each other and find workable solutions to bridge different opinions about political issues. If disinformation becomes such a corrosive agent that it reduces our ability to talk to each other, then society is at risk.[17]

Conspiracy Theories

At the heart of some of the more dangerous examples of disinformation and fake news are conspiracy theories—proposed explanations for what is going on behind the scenes. Some conspiracy theories turn out to be true. For example, for many years it was rumored that tobacco companies buried research showing that cigarette smoking was harmful. In the 1990s tobacco giant Philip Morris finally admitted that smoking could cause cancer.

But many conspiracy theories are just that: theories that people are mysteriously conspiring to keep important information from the public. Famous long-time conspiracy theories include the idea that the US government faked the 1969 moon landing or that the government has proof of the existence of extraterrestrial beings. While these stories have made for some entertaining TV and movies, they are rather harmless.

But in recent years, fueled by social media and fringe online media outlets, conspiracy theories of a much more serious and sinister nature have spread rapidly. Believing stories or ideas that are fictitious or wildly inaccurate is bad enough, but the real danger of misinformation is what people will do with it. Starting in the earliest days of the COVID-19 pandemic, conspiracy theories

A right-wing protester displays signs supporting several COVID conspiracy theories at a rally in Washington, DC, on January 2, 2022. Believing stories that are fictitious or inaccurate is concerning, but the real danger of misinformation is what people will do with it.

about the virus flourished. There were wild tales of its origins, misinformation about how it could harm the body, reluctance to believe how easily it could spread, and unproven and at times dangerous suggestions for how to treat it that were constantly being rebutted by doctors trying to get the truth out to the public. Month after month, the press told stories of families divided by COVID-19 misinformation. In a story reported in *Newsweek* in 2021, Lynne Gibbs of northern England explained that her twenty-four-year-old daughter, Abby, had become so consumed with conspiracy theories about COVID-19 that she backed out of her appointment to get vaccinated. The virus later took Abby's life after three difficult weeks in the intensive care. "Abby was supposed to go the same day as me to have her vaccine, but she was that hooked on conspiracy theories she decided not to go,"[18] her mother says.

One of the reasons people fall for fabricated news stories and disinformation is a concept known as cognitive bias. It refers to the mistakes people make in judgment or reasoning as they try, without realizing they are doing so, to simplify information processing. The brain tends to make shortcuts when it can, as in reading a headline and making up your mind without reading the article. Cognitive bias can also make a person more likely to go along with things or people who are popular, regardless of what they stand for. So, the more "likes" an online story receives or the more attention it is getting, the greater the chances are that it will be seen as positive or at least legitimate, thus giving fake news the whiff of truthfulness.

The Influence of Social Media

Social media platforms such as Facebook carry a lot of news—both fake and real. But they do not report the news. There are no Facebook reporters out there covering campaigns or conflicts abroad, for example. Instead, the platforms aggregate news content, meaning they collect news stories from many other sites and place them in news feeds for users to consume. Story selection

Satire and the News

From TV's *Saturday Night Live* and *The Daily Show* to online sites like the Onion and ClickHole, there is no shortage of outlets dedicated to making fun of the news. While some places satirize or parody actual news events and news makers, others simply make up ridiculous stories and present them in a news format. But the creators of satirical news content run the risk of readers or viewers taking the content seriously and believing the fiction to be fact. That is why it is so important to double-check the source when you read or see something outrageous, even if it looks like it might be real. Aaron Hagey-Mackay, who wrote for the satirical news website the Beaverton, says that despite this risk, satire serves an important function in society. "During periods of social stress, satire offers a 'spoonful of sugar' to hard truths. It can be a source of insight and can convince you to pay attention to things you wouldn't otherwise think about," he said in an interview with *University of Toronto Magazine*. "In a fractured, polarized media landscape, satire can cut through the noise."

Quoted in Scott Anderson, "Satire vs. Fake News," *University of Toronto Magazine*, April 1, 2020. https://magazine.utoronto.ca.

tends to be based on the kinds of news stories the platforms know that individual users search for, read, and share with others. While many articles enter news feeds from legitimate, established news organizations, plenty of others slip through from sites that peddle conspiracy theories, disinformation, and partisan propaganda.

The importance of social media and online news content in the media landscape is undeniable. The Pew Research Center reported in 2021 that eight in ten Americans get some or all of their news online. If most of that news content is coming from reputable news agencies, then it is likely that consumers are getting a mostly factual accounting of events. But a 2020 survey by the Pew Research Center suggests that more than one-third of adults in the United States get at least some of their news from Facebook.

But social media serves another increasingly important role in politics, business, entertainment, and most every other field. Platforms such as Twitter, Instagram, YouTube, and TikTok allow individuals and organizations to reach consumers directly—and without having to work with traditional media organizations to get their messages out. In a story on NPR, Republican strategist and CNN pundit Scott Jennings suggested that journalists are the agents between news makers and news consumers and are not always needed on the campaign trail. He said:

> When I started 20 years ago, you know, you spent a good chunk of every day on campaigns trying to figure out how to get the media to cover whatever you're doing that day. But now, you don't need an intermediary to connect with your supporters . . . [now that] you can connect with your most fervent supporters directly via social media, and campaign email lists, and so on and so forth.[19]

Sponsored Content

Disinformation comes in many forms. Sometimes information can be presented in a misleading way that makes you think it is one thing or that it is coming from a legitimate source, only to be something more ambiguous. Online, TV, and print news stories often must compete with similar content that is not news but rather advertisements presented to look like real news stories. Some advertisers even put banners of actual media operations such as *People* magazine or CNN across the top of these ads to try to further persuade consumers that the content is legitimate. Or they create fictional news sites with names that look like the real thing. Bonnie Patten, executive director of Truth in Advertising.org, told NBC News BETTER that a person has to be "a pretty savvy customer to be able to pick up on the fact that this is not reliable information, that this is someone trying to pitch their product to you in a very disingenuous way."[20]

Usually, in small print at the bottom of these ads are words such as "Sponsored Content" or "Paid Post," which supposedly make it clear that this is an advertisement and not an article. But that information is not obvious at first glance because

Trusting Intuition

Trusting your intuition can be helpful in a lot of situations, but do so with care when it comes to evaluating political and scientific news. A study published in the journal *PLOS One* found that individuals who are especially prone to trusting their intuition—who agreed with statements such as "I trust my gut to tell me what's true and what's not" and who believe that facts in news stories are politically biased—are more likely to accept conspiracy theories and hold inaccurate beliefs. In contrast, individuals who value evidence are less likely to believe fake news.

While there is value in trusting your instincts, it is important to allow evidence, research, and provable facts to guide your acceptance of news stories that you see and hear. On the subject of COVID-19, many people rejected the advice of medical experts because they did not trust the medical community. Political scientist Tom Nichols writes about this, saying, "When the pandemic recedes—and after we have reflected on all of this death and heartbreak—we'll need to recover some perspective and learn once again when to put aside gut instincts and listen to the people who know what they're doing."

Tom Nichols, "Following Your Gut Isn't the Right Way to Go," *The Atlantic*, March 22, 2021. www.theatlantic.com.

advertisers know that readers are more likely to ignore something that obviously looks like an ad as opposed to something that appears to be real news, explains Bart Wojdynski, media professor at the University of Georgia. "I think the advertisers are well aware that they benefit from some ambiguity in the consumer's mind about whether or not it's paid advertising," he said in an article on the Business Insider website. "Otherwise they'd put, in really big letters, right across the top: 'This is a paid advertisement from the company name.' They don't want to do that because they know that consumers habituate themselves to ignore advertising online."[21]

> "I think [sponsored content] advertisers are well aware that they benefit from some ambiguity in the consumer's mind about whether or not it's paid advertising."[21]
>
> —Bart Wojdynski, media professor at the University of Georgia

Claims Without Support

Another way to discern between fact and fiction in the news and advertising is to look for ways certain claims are or are not backed up by evidence or example. Biased language also extends to broad generalizations, unsupported claims, and descriptions that are not always accurate. If something or someone is described as "the worst" or "the best" or "the most dangerous" or is given some other extreme label, it is reasonable to expect some further description or explanation.

Certainly, some things can be described in dramatic terms, but the claims should be supported. For example, Hurricane Katrina is considered the costliest hurricane to hit the United States since 1851, causing about $180 billion in damage. That is a largely indisputable fact against which past and future hurricane damage can be compared. Always be on the lookout for follow-up evidence that backs up the things claimed to be the "best," "worst," "most expensive," or other superlatives.

Hurricane Katrina, which hit the United States in August 2005, caused about $180 billion in damage. This number, while enormous, is an indisputable fact that readers can confidently accept.

Of course, not everything can be quantified. If a claim is made and there is no effort to at least try to make the case for why that claim is true, be skeptical and be aware that the writer or speaker is pushing an agenda. In advertising, companies are obviously pushing an agenda to coax people into spending money on their products or services. But they should still be held accountable for making ambitious claims. Sometimes companies, especially those in the food industry, pay to have research done that supports a particular claim. This gives them some "scientific" evidence to present, even though the study findings may be suspect since the company financed the research. Whenever you see a study touting the health benefits of a particular product, look to see who paid for it and proceed cautiously.

Through the years many companies have had to settle lawsuits when their claims were proved to be false or exaggerated. Kellogg's once claimed that its Frosted Mini-Wheats cereal improved the attentiveness of children who ate it by 20 percent. In a class-action lawsuit, investigators found that even the company-sponsored study did not find that attentiveness improved that much and that most kids in the study showed no improvement at all. The false claim shared in commercials and on the cereal boxes cost Kellogg's $4 million. Not all advertising claims, campaign promises, or theories are bogus, but there is an old saying that is often proved to be accurate: if something sounds too good to be true, it usually is.

CHAPTER FOUR

Fight Back with the Truth

The ancient Greek playwright Euripides once said, "Question everything. Learn something. Answer nothing."[22] For centuries, other great minds have echoed the importance of questioning everything, not because you want to be mistrustful of everyone but because it is often necessary to verify the facts before reaching a decision. But there is more to being a smart news consumer than refusing to take things on face value. There are strategies to improve your media savvy and learn how to recognize media bias and disinformation.

Read Beyond the Headlines

One simple way to avoid being a victim of media bias or disinformation is to read more than the headline on a news story. Headlines have two purposes: to sum up the main idea of a news article and to get people to stop and read the story. And headlines must do all that with just a few words. Unfortunately, this sometimes means that a headline does not accurately reflect what is in the article. In many cases there is no intention to be misleading. It is just that complicated subjects cannot easily be boiled down to a few words. This is often the case with news stories about scientific or medical research.

When scrolling through your news feed or scanning articles elsewhere, take a few minutes to read the stories that catch your eye. Even if you do not read all the way through, you will have a deeper and perhaps more accurate understanding of what the headline was trying to convey.

Consider the Sources of the Information

When reading about studies or statistics, find out who sponsored the study or who is presenting the statistics. Food companies or organizations that represent the food industry frequently sponsor studies to show the health benefits of their products. If you see an article touting the advantages of drinking milk, for example, look to see whether the study was sponsored by the National Dairy Council. If so, this does not mean that the evidence is fraudulent, but it should prompt some further searches to see whether other studies have come to the same conclusion.

Articles touting the advantages of milk might show cute pictures like this one to make readers receptive to their point of view. Consumers should always look for further evidence before believing a claim.

And when someone is quoted in a story or interviewed on TV, think about why this person is being interviewed and what the individual brings to the story. A spokesperson for an elected official is most likely going to say things that make the official look good or that will praise a bill or other cause the official supports. A representative from the fossil fuel industry is going to talk about climate change from the perspective of someone who makes a living from oil and gas, while a fisher will speak from the point of view of someone relying on healthy oceans and fisheries to survive. Bias is not necessarily a bad thing if news stories present a balance of viewpoints and biased claims do not go unchecked.

Look for Context

Seeing video of a violent protest or hearing an edited sound bite can lead you to make a lot of assumptions. It is easy to believe that the short video you saw and heard or even a quote you read in an article accurately sum up a situation. But all too often, the few protesters seen breaking windows or causing trouble are just that—a few people. What may not be shown are the hundreds or thousands of other protesters marching or gathering peacefully. Similarly, when anyone is quoted or has a statement included in a TV or digital news story, remember that it is only a few seconds of what was likely a much longer conversation that will provide context to what was said.

Context refers to the circumstances in which something happens or something is said. When reading or viewing anything that uses bits and pieces of video or short quotes to portray a much larger or more complicated issue, try to find out more about the context. Look for video that shows a wide shot of a crowd in a so-called riot. Are most people peaceful, or has it turned largely violent and chaotic? If you hear sound bites that seem incendiary, find the quote in its entirety or listen for the question that was asked. Having more context is helpful in determining the accuracy of a news story.

Vary Your News Sources

It is common for people to stick with news sources they trust and ones that offer opinions with which they agree. But it is helpful to get news from a variety of sources. Varying your news diet means you are more likely to read stories you might otherwise miss, and you will get opinions that may prompt you to rethink your position on a topic. It is also helpful to get some insight into what opponents think or at least what information they are getting to form their arguments and choices. Knowing different views allows you to engage more reasonably with others and makes you better informed about issues.

Occasionally checking in with news outlets that typically present a slanted or biased take on the news will also help you better understand why people hold such polarized views. Biased news is attractive because it typically presents a cohesive stance on all issues, but in doing so, it often forces facts to fit that narrative or ignores the facts that do not. "We've lost any sense of a common narrative, of a shared reality," says Alan Miller, longtime reporter and founder of the News Literacy Project. "We not only can't agree on what the facts are, we can't even agree on what a fact is."[23]

> "We've lost any sense of a common narrative, of a shared reality. We not only can't agree on what the facts are, we can't even agree on what a fact is."[23]
>
> —Alan Miller, founder of the News Literacy Project

Beware of Buzzwords

Often facts are skewed to fit agendas by the words used to describe or define those facts. Politicians, advertisers, and journalists know that certain words conjure up feelings or associations that similar-meaning words do not. For example, a news outlet that appeals to people with a negative or cynical view of government might refer to a Medicare-for-all plan as "government-run" health care as opposed to "public" health care. Words and phrases such as *government-run* are called buzzwords because they immediately trigger a reaction and are quick and easy for politicians, pundits, and journalists to use when shaping their message.

Many words have lost their more neutral, dictionary meanings because of their continued use in select narratives. For instance, the word *patriot* means someone who loves his or her country and is willing to defend it. But in recent years, *patriot* has often been used to describe someone who is opposed to certain federal laws or policies and actively protests them. Fox News personality Tucker Carlson produced a three-part series about the people who stormed the Capitol on January 6, 2021, and called the series *Patriot Purge*, comparing the protesters to the American colonists who fought for independence against the English monarchy. This was an attempt to align the dangerous and illegal

Fox News personality Tucker Carlson, host of "Tucker Carlson Tonight," has been known to use emotionally laden language to sway viewers when covering controversial news events.

Be Wary of Polls and Surveys

When it comes to politics, especially during election campaigns, a lot of news stories are based on polls and surveys. A poll usually asks one simple question. It is meant to be a quick and easy-to-understand look at a population's preference at a particular point in time. A survey typically asks several questions that allow for more nuanced answers. During a campaign, a survey might explore why voters prefer one candidate over the other or how voters would like elected officials to deal with certain issues.

Polls and surveys can be helpful in revealing more about what people like, what they do not like, and why. But it is important to look beyond the resulting numbers. Knowing more about the survey or poll itself can add to or detract from its credibility. Respected polling organizations usually provide information on how the poll or survey was conducted, how the questions were worded, and how many people were surveyed. Remember that polls, especially during election season, are not guarantees. "It's not a predictor of what's definitely going to happen, but a snapshot of how people are feeling," says Shippensburg University political science professor Alison Dagnes.

Quoted in Sanika Bhargaw, "How Much Should Voters Trust Election Polls?," WHTM-ABC 27, November 4, 2022. www.abc27.com.

actions of those involved in invading the Capitol with colonists overthrowing tyranny. In truth, more than four hundred of them pleaded guilty in court to charges ranging from obstruction of an official proceeding to disorderly conduct to assault.

Many other buzzwords are often used inaccurately. Certain progressive policies, such as protections for LGBTQ students or tighter restrictions on air pollution, are often labeled as "socialist" or "Marxist," even though those philosophies are much more concerned with economic and labor matters than making schools safe for all students and preserving the environment. And when discussing migrants who have crossed the border, but not through official channels, politicians and columnists or commentators often use the terms *undocumented immigrants* or *illegal immigrants* for very specific purposes. *Illegal immigrants* supports efforts to portray these people as criminals, while the term *un-documented immigrants* suggests they are individuals working through a bureaucratic process. *Illegal aliens* is yet another buzz-word meant to dehumanize people crossing the border, because *alien* implies unfamiliarity and reinforces an "us versus them" perspective. US law still includes the phrase, but various media outlets understand that the terminology is not neutral.

As you learn to recognize buzzwords and biased language, you will also start to take notice of news that is presented with-out opinion in responsible, evenhanded language. And when you hear people repeat buzzwords and biased messaging, you can probably get an idea of where they are getting their news. Urging friends and family to find less-biased coverage may be the start of less-contentious discussions down the road.

Venezuelan migrants cross the Rio Bravo near Chihuahua, Mexico, in November 2022. The words chosen to describe these people can influence public opinion of this event.

Support Independent, Nonprofit Journalism

The number of local newspapers is shrinking every year, meaning that many local government decisions and other issues are not being covered and disseminated to the public. Getting a subscription to a local paper or watching a local TV news station gives the support these news outlets need to keep bringing people news from their communities.

Similarly, nonprofit, independent journalism is going on around the world, often bringing unbiased coverage to important subjects. These organizations rely on public support because they are not part of a large media corporation. Some good examples to follow include ProPublica and the *Guardian*. National Public Radio (NPR) and the Public Broadcasting Service (PBS) receive most of their funding from listeners and viewers, though they do receive some government funding and support from foundations and corporate sponsors. However, NPR and PBS consistently strive to provide news that is neither sensational nor one-sided but represents a wide range of opinions presented in formats that welcome critical audiences looking to find the news amid so much media noise.

Call Out Examples of Bias

Many news sites provide opportunities for readers to comment on articles, and many newspapers still run letters from readers. When examples of bias or disinformation appear, they should be identified, and the news outlet and other consumers should be notified. Many news organizations and individual journalists also have a social media presence on Twitter, for example. Calling attention to bias and disinformation in this way may be helpful in making people more accountable for their work.

Consider the Sources

A fundamental principle in news reporting is to present both sides of a story—or if the subject is especially complex, several sides

Recognizing Propaganda

Propaganda refers to the spread of information, rumors, and ideas to either support or harm a particular institution or individual. It is the basis of candidate speeches and campaign advertising. Seeing propaganda for what it is and understanding some of the more common techniques that are used will help make you a wiser and more thoughtful voter. "The media is not to blame for reporting what our politicians say, even if what they say is part of a partisan propaganda campaign. We citizens must be smart and alert enough that we can verify the truth and equally well detect propaganda," *Cincinnati Enquirer* opinion writer Joseph Fox wrote in 2021.

During election campaigns, watch for what is known as the "bandwagon" effect. It aims to make you feel as though you need to join a side or endorse a view because everyone else is doing the same. Celebrity endorsements are also common, as candidates try to get voters to think that if popular performers are on board, their fans should be, too. Keep in mind that just because you like watching a particular actor or athlete, it does not mean that you share their hopes and dreams for the country. Propaganda often succeeds because it appeals to our emotions.

Joseph Fox. "Opinion: Detecting Propaganda Is a Citizen's Responsibility," *Cincinnati (OH) Enquirer*. April 28, 2021. www.cincinnati.com.

should be represented. Say a developer wants to build an apartment complex in an environmentally sensitive area. Balanced, unbiased news coverage would include input from the developer, the people who live in the area, environmentalists familiar with the region, government officials responsible for making decisions about the project, and if possible, individuals who might want to live in the apartments so they can be closer to their jobs.

But if articles and TV news reports include quotes from the developer only or from environmentalists only, then it is fair to label the coverage as biased. Remember that everyone involved in that story has an agenda or priorities that will affect how they feel about the apartment project. The developer wants to make money and promote the business. The environmentalists want to protect the land, water, and wildlife in the area. Neighbors may not want more people and traffic around them. Potential apartment residents want to live there. And government officials may have a range of priorities. Some may support the project because of the tax revenue and economic boost it will provide, while others may be more inclined to protect the environment or keep the area as it is, with fewer residents and cars on the road.

When you read or watch a news story, pay close attention to the voices that are included in the piece and those that are absent. Think about whether you are really getting all sides of the story, since many subjects are complex and involve multiple views.

Look for Wide Coverage

If you see what looks like a bombshell news story about a political candidate or another subject on which people may have very different opinions, take a few minutes to see if other news outlets have the same story. No news organization wants to look like it is missing out on a big story, so if multiple legitimate news outlets carry the same story, you can feel more confident that it is newsworthy.

While this is not a perfect way to identify disinformation, it can often be effective. And though major newspapers, such as the *New York Times* and *Washington Post*, may present news in ways that seem slanted at times, they tend to take a responsible approach to news gathering and presentation. Since every journalist and every news source have some degree of bias, checking a variety of sources can make you aware of the ones that do not distort facts and are more trustworthy in presenting news.

Be a Truth Seeker

Media bias and disinformation will probably never disappear. But if you know how to recognize those efforts to manipulate you, you can be an independent thinker and find the truth amid the noise and distractions. That will make you a better-informed citizen and voter, a smarter and more cautious consumer, and a person who will make decisions based on accurate information. And if you can help others learn to spot examples of media bias and disinformation, maybe those twin menaces to truth and fairness will not be quite so dangerous in the future.

> "Media literacy is literacy in the 21st century. There is this fire hose of information coming at young people, and they have to know how to cope with it."[24]
>
> —Erin McNeill, president of Media Literacy Now

Becoming a savvier consumer of news takes time and a lot of practice. But you can get there by reading news from a variety of sources and paying close attention to headlines, photos, and what is and is not included in stories. It is important to start this practice early, and many schools are now offering classes that address media literacy. Erin McNeill, founder and president of the advocacy group Media Literacy Now, told the *Los Angeles Times* that because it is getting harder to separate fact from fiction in the media and there is so much news easily accessible twenty-four hours a day, students need to develop a whole new set of skills. "Media literacy is literacy in the 21st century," she said. "There is this fire hose of information coming at young people, and they have to know how to cope with it."[24]

Introduction: Be a Smarter News Consumer

1. Quoted in Peter Dizikes, "Study: On Twitter, False News Travels Faster than True Stories," MIT News, March 8, 2018. https://news.mit.edu.
2. Quoted in David Klepper, "How to Read Your Social Media Feeds on Election Day," ABC10, November 7, 2022. www.abc10.com.

Chapter One: What Is News?

3. Lynn Walsh, "Journalist: We Strive for Accuracy in the Context of Known Facts," *Orlando (FL) Sentinel*, September 14, 2017. www.orlandosentinel.com.
4. Quoted in Brett Samuels, "Trump Ramps Up Rhetoric on Media, Calls Press 'the Enemy of the People,'" *The Hill* (Washington, DC), April 5, 2019. https://thehill.com.
5. Quoted in NBC News, *Meet the Press*, January 1, 2017. www.nbcnews.com.
6. Quoted in Max Witynski, "False Balance in News Coverage of Climate Change Makes It Harder to Address the Crisis," Northwestern Now, July 22, 2022. https://news.northwestern.edu.
7. Quoted in Witynski, "False Balance in News Coverage of Climate Change Makes It Harder to Address the Crisis."
8. Robert H. Shmerling, "Careful! Health News Headlines Can Be Deceiving," *Staying Healthy* (blog), Harvard Health Publishing, November 12, 2021. www.health.harvard.edu.
9. Better Business Bureau, "Watch Out for Clickbait Scams Following a Tragedy," January 27, 2020. www.bbb.org.

Chapter Two: Biased Language and Spin

10. Quoted in Paul Farhi, "Sean Hannity Thinks People Can Tell the Difference Between News and Opinion: Hold on a Moment," *Washington Post*, March 28, 2017. www.washingtonpost.com.
11. Quoted in Katy Steinmetz, "'A War of Words.' Why Describing the George Floyd Protests as 'Riots' Is So Loaded," *Time*, June 8, 2020. https://time.com.

12. Quoted in Tanner Stening, "Just How Biased Is the Mainstream Media?," News @ Northeastern, September 16, 2022. http://news .northeastern.edu.

Chapter Three: Disinformation

13. Quoted in Nicole Carroll, "What It's like Covering Election Day at *USA Today*: See What Happens Hour by Hour in Our Newsroom," *USA Today*, November 10, 2022. www.usatoday.com.
14. Quoted in Goodreads, "Vladimir Lenin Quotes," 2022. www.good reads.com.
15. Quoted in MSU Today, "MSU Expert: How Misinformation and Disinformation Influence Elections," October 20, 2022. https://msuto day.msu.edu.
16. Quoted in Samuels, "Trump Ramps Up Rhetoric on Media, Calls Press 'the Enemy of the People.'"
17. Quoted in MSU Today, "MSU Expert."
18. Quoted in Khaleda Rahman, "Mom, 24, 'Hooked on Conspiracy Theories' Dies After Rejecting COVID Shot," *Newsweek*, October 24, 2021. www.newsweek.com.
19. Quoted in Danielle Kurtzleben, "Republicans Have Long Feuded with the Mainstream Media. Now Many Are Shutting Them Out," NPR, August 7, 2022. www.npr.org.
20. Quoted in Herb Weisbaum, "How Fake News Stories About Meghan Markle and Kelly Clarkson Are Used to Sell Diet Pills and Wrinkle Creams," NBC News BETTER, October 19, 2019. www.nbcnews .com.
21. Quoted in Will Heilpern, "How 'Deceptive' Sponsored News Articles Could Be Tricking Readers—Even with a Disclosure Message," Business Insider, March 17, 2016. www.businessinsider.com.

Chapter Four: Fight Back with the Truth

22. "Euripedes: Quotes." GoodReads. www.goodreads.com.
23. "'I Want to Be Part of a Society That Gets Things Right': *Los Angeles Times* Features New Push for News Literacy," News Literacy Project, October 27, 2022. www.newslit.org.
24. Quoted in James Rainey, "'Media Literacy' Advocates Push to Create Savvier Consumers of News and Information," *Los Angeles Times*, October 26, 2022. www.latimes.com.

Books

Ben Boyington, *The Media and Me: A Guide to Critical Media Literacy for Young People*. New York: Triangle Square, 2022.

Joyce Grant, *Can You Believe It? How to Spot Fake News and Find the Facts*. Toronto, Canada: Kids Can, 2022.

Renee Hobbs, *Media Literacy in Action: Questioning the Media*. Lanham, MD: Rowman & Littlefield, 2021.

Marcus E. Howard, *How Journalists and the Public Shape Our Democracy*, Atlanta: Georgia Humanities Council, 2019.

Jennifer LaGarde and Darren Hudgins, *Developing Digital Detectives: Essential Lessons for Discerning Fact from Fiction in the "Fake News" Era*. Toronto, Canada: University of Toronto Press, 2021.

Jeffrey Wilhelm et al., *Fighting Fake News: Teaching Students to Identify and Interrogate Information Pollution*. Thousand Oaks, CA: Corwin, 2023.

Internet Sources

Anti-Defamation League, "Conspiracy Theories and How to Help Family and Friends Who Believe Them," August 23, 2022. www.adl.org.

New York Times, "Behind the Journalism: How the *Times* Works," November 1, 2022. www.nytimes.com.

James Rainey, "'Media Literacy' Advocates Push to Create Savvier Consumers of News and Information," *Los Angeles Times*, October 26, 2022. www.latimes.com.

Websites

Glossary: The Language of News Literacy, Stony Brook University Center for News Literacy
https://digitalresource.center/glossary-language-news-literacy
This glossary page on the Stony Brook University Center for

News Literacy website includes definitions and examples of media terminology ranging from *accountability* to *verification*. It helps explain the differences between news and publicity, direct and indirect evidence, and much more.

Fairness and Accuracy in Reporting (FAIR)
www.fair.org
FAIR is a media watchdog group. Its Media Literacy Guide lists questions news consumers should ask about the stories they read and watch. The group also critiques actual news stories, looking at the use of anonymous sources, story point of view, and news organization funding sources.

Misinformation, Disinformation, and Propaganda, Cornell University Library
https://guides.library.cornell.edu/evaluate_news
This site includes several short but helpful guides on subjects such as fake news, evaluating news sources, and identifying source bias. The site also contains a long list of media evaluation resources to understand more about how news organizations function and how to become more media savvy.

News Literacy Project
https://newslit.org
Educators use the expansive resources from this site for courses and lesson plans on media literacy and recognizing bias and misinformation. But anyone can access the guides, newsletters, and tips for becoming a more knowledgeable consumer of news and information.

After graduating from the University of Oregon, James Roland became a newspaper reporter, primarily focused on education. He later became a magazine writer and editor as well as an author of more than a dozen books. He and his wife, Heidi, have three children, Chris, Alexa, and Carson.

LONGWOOD PUBLIC LIBRARY
800 Middle Country Road
Middle Island, NY 11953
(631) 924-6400
longwoodlibrary.org

LIBRARY HOURS

Monday-Friday	9:30 a.m. - 9:00 p.m.
Saturday	9:30 a.m. - 5:00 p.m.
Sunday (Sept-June)	1:00 p.m. - 5:00 p.m.